101 Silly Things Employees Do To Sabotage Success

Richard Baisner

Richard Chang Associates, Inc.
Publications Division
Irvine, California

101 Stupid Things Employees Do To Sabotage Success

Richard Baisner

Library of Congress Catalog Card Number
97-69478

© 1998, Richard Chang Associates, Inc.
Printed in the United States of America

All rights reserved. No part of this publication may be reproduced, stored in a retrieval system, or transmitted in any form or by any means, electronic, mechanical, photocopying, recording, or otherwise, without the prior written permission of the publisher.

ISBN 1-883553-97-0

Editors: Bill Foster and Karen Johnson
Reviewer: Shirley Codrey
Graphic Layout: Richard Baisner and Christina Slater
Cover Design: Dena Putnam

RICHARD CHANG ASSOCIATES

Richard Chang Associates, Inc.
Publications Division
15265 Alton Parkway, Suite 300
Irvine, CA 92618
(800) 756-8096   (714) 727-7477
Fax (714) 727-7007
www.richardchangassociates.com

About The Author

Richard Baisner is the Materials Development Team Leader of Richard Chang Associates, Inc. (RCA), where he assists in the development of RCA's organizational improvement training programs, presentations, and seminars. Richard also serves as a reviewer for many guidebooks from RCA's Practical Guidebook Collection. In addition, he is known for his expertise in office automation, systems documentation, and process improvement using computer system technologies.

Acknowledgments

This book would not have been possible without "stupid" and useful input from family, friends, and colleagues. Special thanks go to Doug Dalziel, Denise Jeffrey, Erin O'Slaherty, and all the colleagues who unknowingly contributed to this book.

Table of Contents

Introduction viii

1. Productivity Pitfalls 1
   #1 The Ramblin' Man
   #2 Bogus Focus
   #3 When The Cat's Away
   #4 A Day Of Surfing
   #5 It's Who You Know
   #6 Monster Projects
   #7 Have You Had Your Break Today?
   #8 The Problem Child
   #9 Feast Or Famine
   #10 Game Over
   #11 Rest And Relaxation

2. Policy Perils 15
   #12 Know Any Good Lawyers?
   #13 From Riches To Rags
   #14 Let's Get Physical
   #15 A Fool And His Money Are Soon Partying
   #16 Eureka!
   #17 Hanky Panky
   #18 Perks And Quirks
   #19 A Pirate's Life For Me
   #20 Syntax Errors
   #21 Bedtime For Bonzo
   #22 Under The Weather

3. Communication Catastrophes 29
   #23 Position Secured
   #24 Joker's Wild
   #25 A Comedy Of Errors
   #26 Can You Repeat The Part After "Are You Getting All This?"

#27 Messy Messages
#28 Confessional Help
#29 Tug-Of-War
#30 Born To Be Mild
#31 The Yankee Doodler
#32 You've Got Mail!
#33 Speaking Your Mind
#34 Skeletons In The Closet

4. Behavioral Blunders 43
#35 Pound For Pound
#36 Hey, I Just Work Here!
#37 Temper, Temper
#38 Got Any Change?
#39 Doubting Thomas
#40 Another Monday ... Oh Joy!
#41 The Unhappy Camper
#42 Are We Having Fun Yet?
#43 Be Like Me
#44 Wake-Up Calls
#45 5:00? I'm Outta Here!

5. Habitual Habits 57
#46 Ill-Fated
#47 Garbage In, Garbage Out
#48 Putting Off Today What You Can Do Tomorrow
#49 If You Snooze, You Lose
#50 Clearance Denied
#51 Paperboy
#52 I Wanna Hold Your Hand
#53 Behind The Times
#54 Well ... I Forget
#55 Analysis-Paralysis
#56 All Work And No Play

6. Ethical Enigmas 71
#57 Now You See Me, Now You Don't
#58 Not Enough Hours In A Day
#59 Fringe Benefits
#60 If At First You Don't Succeed, Pry Pry Again
#61 Numbers Don't Lie, But Do You?
#62 Phone Home
#63 Network Opportunities
#64 Fast Food Take Out
#65 Sabotaging Success
#66 I Know Something You Don't Know
#67 Double-Time

7. Teamwork Troubles 85
#68 Don't Test Me!
#69 Thank You! Thank You! I'm Here All Week
#70 Teams Are For Sports
#71 Not Another Meeting!
#72 What A Concept!
#73 Let Them Eat Cake
#74 Does He Still Work Here?
#75 Now Drop And Give Me Twenty!
#76 Absolutely, 100%, Not Guilty
#77 Vows Of Silence
#78 No Assistance

8. Management Mishaps 99
#79 On A Need-To-Know Basis
#80 Out Of Sight, Out Of Mind
#81 What Do You Mean I Can't Take Criticism?!
#82 Promotional Material
#83 So, How's Life At The Top?
#84 You've Disrespected The Family
#85 The Boss's Pet
#86 Speak Now, Or Forever Hold Your Peace
#87 Head Over Heels
#88 Power To The People!
#89 Party Fowls

9. Simply Stupid 113
#90 The Sound Of Music
#91 Suitability
#92 Fashionably Late
#93 Quick And Dirty
#94 Hook, Line, And Sinker
#95 Hostel Takeovers
#96 Back Me Up On This
#97 Hit And Run
#98 Jack-Of-All-Trades
#99 I've Been Asking Myself That For Years
#100 Just Like Home
#101 Prankly My Dear ...

Summary 127

Introduction

*"Success in almost any field depends more on
energy and drive than it does on intelligence.
This explains why we have so many stupid leaders."*

Sloan Wilson

When forced to confess, most employees admit stories about stupid things they've done while on the job. However, is it necessary to learn the hard way, one blunder after another?

Outstanding employees work hard to improve their skills, behaviors, and communication skills. This book will make your progress easier. Now you can avoid doing those stupid things that always seem to appear on your performance review.

Maybe you've just joined a new organization and you want to excel. Perhaps you've been working at the same organization for many years, but still haven't achieved your goals. Almost anyone can benefit from reading this book. New employees, team leaders, and even managers can use this book to boost their own productivity and remind themselves of the little things that got them where they are today.

The guidelines in this book are not a set of rigid, exact rules. No two organizations are alike, so you need to be flexible in adapting the success strategies to your own unique situation. It's a reference tool designed for browsing and for enjoying. Consider this book as your own personal policy manual.

After all, you probably spend more time at work than you do with your friends and family. Why not make the best of it? We feel it's far easier to learn when you can also laugh.

So, let *101 Stupid Things Employees Do To Sabotage Success* help you better appreciate life at the office and those you work with.

Chapter 1
Productivity Pitfalls

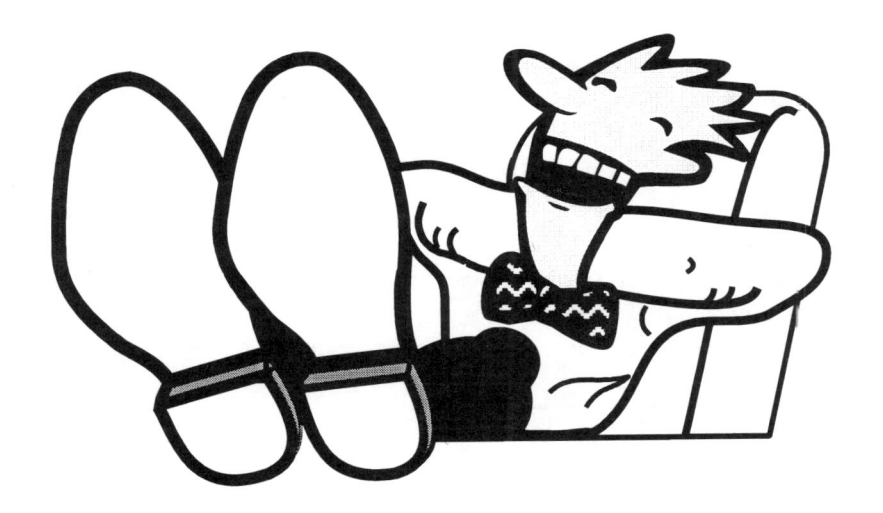

#1 The Ramblin' Man

One of your coworkers constantly distracts you at your desk with long drawn-out stories and boring anecdotes. By laughing at random and appearing interested, you inspire him to return time after time.

What's Wrong?

- 📢 Both of you are being unproductive.

- 📢 He thinks you have nothing better to do.

- 📢 The constant interruptions keep you from focusing on your tasks.

- 📢 His life will soon become your life.

- 📢 When he shows up on your next family vacation, you'll have no one to blame but yourself.

Say, do you mind if I call you at home tonight?

Some Success Strategies:

Send nonverbal clues such as glancing at your watch, faking a yawn, slowly backing away, or focusing your eyes elsewhere. If that doesn't work, try ending the conversation with statements such as "Well, back to the ol' salt mine," or "Gee whiz! Look at the time." If he simply doesn't get it, tell him you don't have time to socialize, or that others are starting to complain. Still no success? File a formal complaint with his immediate supervisor.

#2 Bogus Focus

Your supervisor asked you to generate the sales report for the weekly staff meeting. As a finishing touch, you displayed your creativity by adding a full-color cover that only took a few hours. It was never looked at.

What's Wrong?

- Time and resources were wasted.
- You displayed poor judgment.
- She didn't ask for it.
- You come across as a show-off.
- You're not focused on end-results.
- The starving artist position is looking better and better.
- It'll end up in the circular file.

Some Success Strategies:

Clarify up-front what the end result of your report should be. Don't make assumptions that may cause rework. Ask where you should focus your attention (e.g., accuracy, cost savings, making the deadline). Avoid varying from organizational standards unless it's perceived as beneficial or an improvement by those in charge of the project. Study good examples of outputs and try to produce similar results.

#3 When The Cat's Away

Whenever top management leaves the office for a business trip, you've noticed your trusty comrades celebrate the occasion wholeheartedly. You attempt to ignore them, as your project deadline rapidly approaches.

What's Wrong?

- You can't concentrate.
- The entire organization suffers.
- Management might come back unexpectedly.
- You're supporting an "us-versus-them" mentality.
- Constant supervision is obviously needed.
- You're considering calling the police to break up the party.

Some Success Strategies:

No one likes to be a party pooper, so try making sarcastic remarks to the offenders such as "I wish I had your job!" Act like a smart business owner and help others recognize the fact that they are only hurting themselves. Inspire others to take initiative and don't let the performance of others pull you down. If there's a lack of direction, ask your supervisor to post a to-do list with deadlines. Nothing doing? Inform management anonymously or in person.

#4 A Day Of Surfing

You've been given access to the Internet to search for business-related information, but you've found yourself spending too much time on-line. Half the time you can't find what you're looking for, and the other half is spent staring at the hourglass cursor.

What's Wrong?

- It's unproductive.

- You might be looking for information that doesn't even exist.

- You get frustrated.

- You're lost in the web.

- You've surfed all around the world, but only came back with a few good cooking recipes.

Some Success Strategies:

Don't go on-line if you're not sure what you're looking for. You're just asking to get lost. Avoid being sidetracked by advertisements or links to web sites unrelated to what you're trying to find. Learn how to use the appropriate Usenet newsgroups and search engines. When you're researching old information, remember to check the archive sections. If data transmissions are slow, log in during off-peak hours or purchase faster communication equipment. Disable unnecessary web page graphics through your web browser program. Take an Internet class or ask a guru for advice.

#5 It's Who You Know

One of your more "unusual" friends was layed off from his job recently, and has repeatedly asked you if there are openings in your department. Even though it's against your better judgment, you give him a high recommendation.

What's Wrong?

- There's probably a good reason why he was let go in the first place.
- You'll get blamed if he screws up.
- You're not acting in the best interest of the company.
- It's unfair to candidates who are better qualified.
- It might ruin your friendship.
- It's biased.
- He might become *your* boss.

Some Success Strategies:

Don't let personal friends stand in the way of your own success. Put the well-being of the company first. Give your honest opinion when you're being used as a reference. Suggest that your friend look for a job elsewhere by looking into classified ads, the Internet, and job agencies. Maybe refer him to one of those "clown schools." Tell him you've heard that the pay is pretty good once you graduate. Ask yourself, "If I owned my own business, would I hire him?"

#6 Monster Projects

Your inbox seems to grow overnight. The stress causes your brain to go into a "shut down" mode. Since you don't know where to begin, you simply don't.

What's Wrong?

- You're falling further behind.
- Management claims you don't work well under pressure.
- Nothing gets accomplished.
- You appear slow and unproductive.
- It's demonstrating a lack of planning.
- You're about to be eaten alive.

Some Success Strategies:

When faced with competing deadlines, prioritize your tasks with your manager. Ask for extra help if needed. Break large projects into smaller, more manageable tasks. Try to work smarter, not harder! Avoid interruptions by arranging to come in during off hours or by isolating yourself in a quiet office. Remember that when you're in a hole, it's best to stop digging.

#7 Have You Had Your Break Today?

Your morning routine consists of getting coffee, reading the paper, getting a snack, and taking a break. After lunch, your schedule is filled with reading the bulletin board, preparing for happy hour, and completing your time sheet.

What's Wrong?

☞ You're virtually worthless.

☞ Management will start questioning the need for your position.

☞ No one can locate you when problems occur.

☞ Tracking you down makes others unproductive.

☞ For convenience, they'll move your workstation into the break room.

Some Success Strategies:

Use your authorized break times appropriately. Plan structured breaks throughout your day and remain available. Get in the habit of multitasking and avoid making repeated and/or unnecessary trips. Try keeping track of your activity every hour and analyze the results. You may be surprised at what you find! Solicit feedback about how others view your performance, and then get back to work!

#8 The Problem Child

You have a lot on your mind recently, and can't help but be distracted at work. You're constantly being bombarded with phone calls from bill collectors, plumbers, doctors, and psychiatrists. Others are starting to notice your lack of performance.

What's Wrong?

- You've got some real problems on your hands.
- Everyone's worried about you.
- You can't focus on your work.
- You're falling further behind.
- Ulcers are no fun.
- A nervous breakdown could be right around the corner.

Some Success Strategies:

If at all possible, leave your problems at home. Take some time off if needed to get pressing personal issues under control. Control outside interference at work by screening outside calls and unexpected visitors. Maybe schedule an appointment with a counselor. Set priorities and overcome personal challenges one at a time. Remember that most things people worry about never happen!

#9 Feast Or Famine

Your workload often comes in phases ... one minute you're filing your fingernails, the next you're bombarded with urgent projects, upcoming deadlines, and yelling bosses.

What's Wrong?

- Your workload is off-balance.
- You're not planning properly.
- The existing processes are unstable.
- You aren't utilizing slow times to your advantage.
- Before long you'll be going through a famine permanently.

Some Success Strategies:

Install better lines of communication between you, your customers, and your suppliers in order to anticipate when future hand-offs will take place. Request access to others' schedules and calendars. Ask them to hand off any available work in portions instead of all at once. Be proactive by using slow times to plan in advance and to streamline current processes.

#10 Game Over

You could play those games on that new computer for hours on end. Come to think of it, you typically do! You'd like to believe you're improving your problem-solving abilities, but in reality you're not playing with a full deck.

What's Wrong?

♣ Annoyed coworkers will start to complain.

♣ You're wasting valuable company time.

♣ They might replace your computer with a typewriter.

♣ You may be violating company policy.

♣ You should focus on getting a high score on your performance review instead.

♣ You'll wear out your mouse.

Some Success Strategies:

Assuming you have finished all of your work, show initiative by asking others if they need assistance. Buy a computer or a video game system to keep you entertained at home. Make your job more exciting by making a game out of it. Post a "playing while on break" sign if you want to use your computer for such activities during breaks. Quickly hide the screen when you hear someone coming.

#11 Rest And Relaxation

You worked long and hard to get that promotion, and now you believe your new position entitles you to various managerial tasks such as napping, daydreaming, and vacation planning.

What's Wrong?

- You're a heel.
- Others start following in your footsteps.
- Management might give you the boot.
- You may as well go home.
- You're causing others to miss deadlines.
- They're considering giving you two desks (one for each foot).

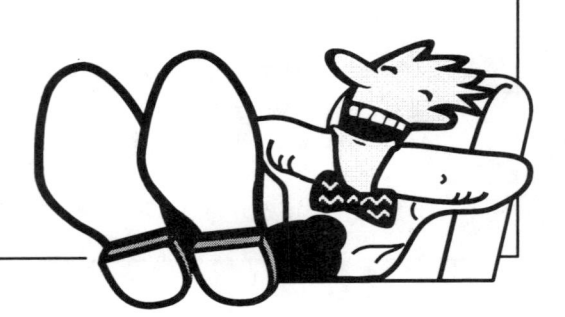

Some Success Strategies:

Remember that success is a journey—not a destination. You are expected to be more responsible, not less. Pull yourself up by your bootstraps and openly accept new opportunities and challenges. Be fair to your coworkers by doing your share of the workload. Renew a sense of purpose for yourself by setting short- and long-term goals. Be motivated. Actively seek ways to be further promoted.

Chapter 2

Policy Perils

#12 Know Any Good Lawyers?

Piece by piece, you've managed to convert your home garage into a plush office complete with a computer network, phone equipment, and a fax machine. The only hard part was sneaking it out to your car and removing the serial numbers.

What's Wrong?

- It's a serious crime.
- You may get caught.
- Your whole career could be destroyed.
- The inventory system gets out of sync.
- You're a tightwad.
- You might not like your new inmates, but they might surely like you.

Some Success Strategies:

Never take company property home without permission. If it's just an old chair that no one will miss, then there's no reason why you can't buy your own. Consider purchasing inexpensive office equipment at swap meets and going-out-of-business sales. If you need to borrow company equipment for business use, be sure to get permission from the appropriate person and that you bring it back on time.

#13 From Riches To Rags

By popular demand, your organization implemented a business casual day. You go all-out by growing a beard, cutting holes in your jeans, and wearing tye-dyes.

What's Wrong?

- It causes distractions.
- You may ruin casual day for everyone.
- You're setting unprecedented standards.
- It's creating an atmosphere unsuitable for business.
- You're not dressed for success.
- Coworkers greet you with a peace sign.
- Baby, this just isn't groovy.

Some Success Strategies:

If you have to question whether or not an article of clothing is appropriate for the office, it's best not to risk it. Save it for the company picnic. Refer to your organization's policy manual, or ask the office manager what is appropriate and what is not. Pay attention to what your supervisor wears and dress similarly (unless his wardrobe consists of clip-on ties, polyester pants, and bell-bottoms).

#14 Let's Get Physical

You have a nemesis at the office you simply don't get along with. Sometimes tempers flare between the two of you, and you feel like throwing a paper weight in her general direction.

What's Wrong?

- You could seriously injure someone.
- She might sock you with a court case.
- Or with a briefcase.
- A broken nose is painful.
- You need professional help.
- Violence is no way to solve problems.
- Can't we all just get along?

Go Ahead... MAKE MY DAY

Some Success Strategies:

Discuss disagreements rationally and calmly. Don't always try to get in the last word. When things get heated, leave the area for a few minutes. Apologize when you lose self-control. Propose and seek ways to support one another on work issues and personal matters. If needed, confer with a third party to settle disputes. Build strong relationships with coworkers by looking for a "common ground" on which to stand. Install a punching bag in your garage, and use it when you get home.

#15 A Fool And His Money Are Soon Partying

On your lunch hour, you customarily relax with a few cocktails at the local bar. Everyone there knows your favorite drink—the next one.

What's Wrong?

- You become careless and may cause an accident.
- Others avoid you.
- You're an embarrassment.
- Poor decisions are made.
- Your productivity decreases.
- There's little nutrition in beernuts and pretzels.
- You might stumble across your termination papers when you get back.

Some Success Strategies:

Never use drugs or alcohol which could adversely affect job performance. You may be jeopardizing the safety of other employees or company property! If you find work to be stressful, find other ways to relax. Avoid going to places where alcohol is served. Take a walk, go to the gym, or read a book on your lunch hour instead. If you think you may have a drinking problem, put down the bottle and seek professional help.

#16 Eureka!

Recently you haven't had the time or the willpower to take a shower. After all, what you do in your spare time is nobody's business but your own.

What's Wrong?

- It's gross negligence.
- You're embarrassing yourself and those around you.
- There's a certain air about you.
- People avoid being around you.
- It's unsanitary.
- Nearby coworkers can't concentrate.
- Basically, you stink.

Some Success Strategies:

Allocate the appropriate amount of time each morning for proper hygiene. Otherwise, bring a "care pack" with you to work, complete with deodorant, toothbrush, gum, razor, comb, etc. Clean up in the company bathroom or in your car if necessary. Try wearing cologne, perfume, or both.

#17 Hanky Panky

You consider your subtle innuendos, whistling, and playful pinching as "good-natured fun." Your photo was distributed along with the new sexual harassment policy.

What's Wrong?

- Others are constantly having to watch their backs, *literally*.
- You're asking for a slap in the face.
- Your behavior is out of hand.
- Marriage is not within your grasp.
- It's immature, offensive, and unprofessional.
- You need a cold shower.

Some Success Strategies:

Don't put yourself in these types of predicaments. Never behave in a manner that could be perceived as harassing, coercing, or intimidating to others. Save this type of behavior for after hours—when you're at home by yourself. Limit your physical contact with others to shaking hands. Don't use phrases such as "stud," "honey," "doll," or "hunk." Avoid making comments referring to people's clothes, bodies, or looks.

#18 Perks And Quirks

To earn extra money, you're currently moonlighting with one of your organization's competitors. You have no qualms about sharing trade secrets and inside information for personal gain.

What's Wrong?

- 💰 Security will be tightened.
- 💰 Your organization's profits suffer.
- 💰 You drive the competition single-handedly.
- 💰 It's disloyal.
- 💰 You're creating a conflict of interest.
- 💰 Traitors get no respect.

Some Success Strategies:

Never communicate confidential or proprietary information beyond those who have a business need to know. Remain faithful to your organization. Decline gifts from vendors and companies that have an outside concern with your organization. If you have any doubts, always disclose anything that may be considered a conflict of interest to management.

#19 A Pirate's Life For Me

"Borrowing" commercial computer programs from work and installing them on your home computer is one of your more favorite hobbies.

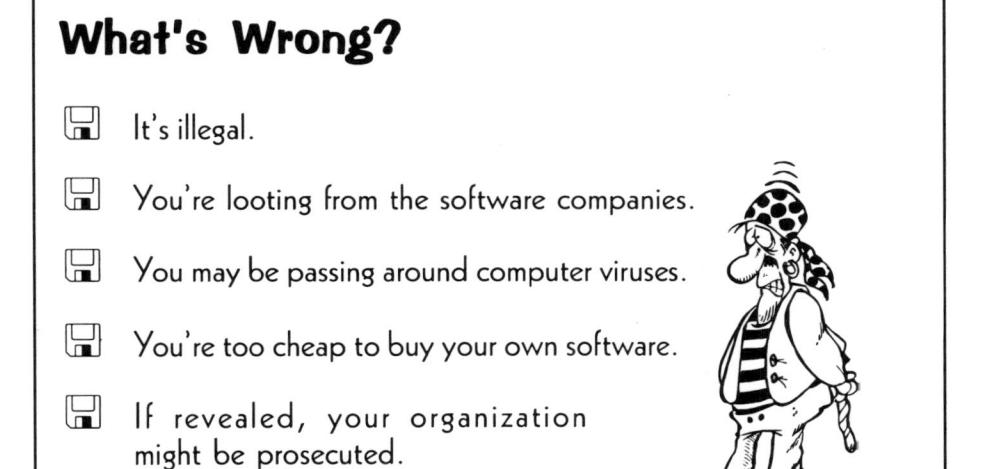

What's Wrong?

- 💾 It's illegal.
- 💾 You're looting from the software companies.
- 💾 You may be passing around computer viruses.
- 💾 You're too cheap to buy your own software.
- 💾 If revealed, your organization might be prosecuted.
- 💾 They'll make you walk the plank.

Some Success Strategies:

Don't make illegal copies of commercial software on your home computer, or on work computers that aren't licensed to use the software. Become familiar with the "End User License Agreement" or similar documentation that comes with the original documentation and take it seriously. If you work from home often, ask for authorization to purchase a separate license for your home computer.

#20 Syntax Errors

When things don't go your way, you have a tendency of swearing in order to get your point across and stress your displeasure. You believe cursing and intimidation are proper communication techniques.

What's Wrong?

?# You sound uneducated.

?# It hurts people's feelings.

?# You sound offensive and unprofessional.

?# Swearing can be considered harassment.

?# People stop listening to you.

?# And you still wonder why a bar of soap was included in your severance package.

Some Success Strategies:

Think about what you're saying before you say it, and consider a better way to get your point across. Keep your conversations friendly and under control. Pay close attention to the language used by others in the workplace. If you're unsure if certain words are acceptable for the office, ask the human resources manager. At least switch foul words with ones that are less offensive.

#21 Bedtime For Bonzo

You've discovered that time flies by quickly at work ... when you're unconscious. You place a report in front of you, pretend to be reading it, and shut your eyes. At least you're still available for emergencies.

What's Wrong?

- You forgot to bring a pillow.
- You're unproductive and abusing company time.
- You're a dreamer.
- Personal motivation is lacking.
- There's a rude awakening in the works.
- Your snoring keeps everyone else awake.

Some Success Strategies:

If you have problems staying alert on the job, you obviously need more sleep. Wake up and smell the coffee. Take a brisk walk to get more oxygen and keep the body alert. Strike up a conversation with a coworker, or turn on the radio. Sit up straight—it can actually increase your attentiveness. Consider changing your diet and getting into an exercise program. Best of all, ask your supervisor for more responsibilities during slow periods.

#22 Under The Weather

You're regarded as highly dependable at your job. Even a nasty cold won't stop you from coming in. Besides, you enjoy hoarding your sick days for those extended vacations.

What's Wrong?

✖ The whole office gets infected.

✖ You need a taste of your own medicine.

✖ Without rest, you'll get even worse.

✖ When coworkers get sick, they'll hunt you down.

✖ You're a pill.

✖ Sick days are meant to be taken—not to be saved up as an early retirement fund.

Some Success Strategies:

Leave your coughing, wheezing, and other unidentifiable guttural emissions at home. If being out significantly affects production, prepare now by suggesting that your supervisor develop contingency plans. Request that your department cross-trains one another for these types of situations. Document your work procedures step by step so others can quickly fill in when needed. If possible, arrange to work at home.

Chapter 3
Communication Catastrophes

#23 Position Secured

You're often reluctant to share your tricks of the trade and job procedures with coworkers. Being the hub of information gives you a sense of power and job security.

What's Wrong?

- They often call you in on weekends to fix things.
- Assumptions made by uninformed coworkers when you're not available can lead to disaster.
- You may be perceived as a know-it-all.
- To be promotable, you must be replaceable.
- They consider your brain a part of the company's intellectual property.

Some Success Strategies:

Keep accurate, detailed documentation on how you do your work processes, and organize the information into a user-friendly procedure manual. Let others know where it is so they can refer to it when you're away. Develop others by delegating tasks and sharing knowledge whenever possible. Remain accessible to people who may need advice or aid from you.

#24 Joker's Wild

You love sharing off-color jokes with your coworkers. But, for some reason, you always seem to have the last laugh.

What's Wrong?

- 📢 Your jokes may be inappropriate for the office.
- 📢 No one takes you seriously.
- 📢 You won't like management's punchline.
- 📢 It may be perceived as offensive and insulting.
- 📢 Some jokes can be considered harassment.
- 📢 You're such a card, you should be dealt with.

Some Success Strategies:

Everyone loves a good joke now and then—in good taste. Use your best judgment in regards to time, place, and appropriateness. If you're in a meeting or on the phone, pay attention to the overall mood of the conversation and adjust accordingly. Humor can act as a great icebreaker, but it's safer to wait for someone else to initiate it. Remember that jokes directed at yourself are usually the safest (and often the most humorous).

#25 A Comedy Of Errors

Grammar was never one of your strong points. Hence, your memos are constantly riddled with errors, typos, and misinformation.

What's Wrong?

- You were probably asleep during English 101.

- It creates mass confusion.

- The number of inaccuracies causes you to look careless.

- Your associates don't take your memos seriously.

- It causes rework.

- Your writing skills are a reflection of your professional skills.

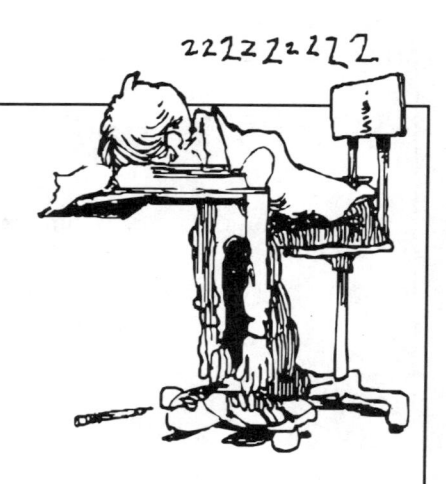

Some Success Strategies:

Whenever possible, run documents through a spell-checker and/or a grammar-checker, especially when they're being read outside the organization. Be careful! Pay close attention to details. Strive to make your memos concise and to the point. Have someone else proof your work before distribution. Take a course in business writing, or read a book on effective writing skills. Study how others at your organization write correspondence and follow their lead. Read your memos out loud to yourself. If it doesn't sound right, it's probably wrong.

#26 Can You Repeat The Part After "Are You Getting All This?"

You met with your supervisor to discuss a new assignment, but left somewhat confused about what you were supposed to do next. To avoid embarrassment, you returned to your desk to somehow figure it out on your own.

What's Wrong?

- You're creating unnecessary work for yourself.
- You could spend hours working on the wrong thing.
- He'll be outraged when you come back a day later with questions.
- His time is wasted repeating himself.
- You give a new definition to guesswork.

Some Success Strategies:

Before going into your supervisor's office or into an information-sharing meeting, make it a habit of bringing a pad of paper with you for taking notes. Jot down any potential ideas to share or questions to ask. Prepare a project debriefing form in advance containing all the pertinent questions to ensure that all decisions, action items, and responsibilities are clearly defined and summarized. If you get confused, don't feel intimidated to ask for clarification.

#27 Messy Messages

Everyone dreads listening to your voice mails. They seem to go on forever! People tend to lose patience and delete your messages halfway through.

What's Wrong?

- You're not focusing on key points.
- Important information is being erased.
- Details are getting lost in the shuffle.
- It's wasting everyone's time.
- You drive note-takers crazy.
- Message space is not unlimited.
- There was never a need for call blocking...until now.

Some Success Strategies:

Organize your thoughts in advance. Include one subject per voice mail and preface it with a subject line summarizing the contents. Don't send messages to those who don't need them, or to people around the corner from you. Keep the message brief and to the point. If you have a lot of information to share at once, set up a conference call or distribute a memo.

#28 Confessional Help

You just made a serious blunder that will ultimately cost the company time, money, and resources. You panic and attempt to destroy any evidence linking you to the crime.

What's Wrong?

- You can't sleep at night.
- Without immediate notification, the problem could potentially get worse.
- Management may be able to remedy the situation easily.
- The exact same thing may happen to someone else.
- Mistakes are often a blessing in disguise.
- They might dust for fingerprints.

Some Success Strategies:

Learn to take responsibility and admit your mistakes. You may be rewarded for your honesty. Use mistakes as a learning process, and plan ways to avoid repeating them. When communicating bad news, consider softening the blow by adding humor. If your supervisor is known to have a bad temper, consider alternative means of notification such as voice mail, through one of his peers, or from another country.

#29 Tug-Of-War

You quickly agree to take on side projects from other departments without consideration of your current workload. Basically, you're a people pleaser and find it hard to say no.

What's Wrong?

- You set yourself up to do the impossible.
- You run around in circles.
- Soon you'll be missing your own deadlines.
- People will constantly take advantage of you.
- You'll resent them for it.
- If you don't perform, you let others down.
- They may make you an inter-department "floater."

Some Success Strategies:

Don't accept unrealistic time demands imposed upon you, or overcommit yourself to unreasonable requests. Empower yourself to say "No" when appropriate. Maintain an ongoing list of your projects, and show it to those requesting your time. Negotiate deadlines, resources, and budgets whenever possible. Remember that it's better to do less well, than more poorly.

#30 Born To Be Mild

You're often running personal errands for your supervisor and doing things that aren't in your job description. After you did his grocery shopping last Christmas, you ended up having your holiday dinner at your desk to catch up on your "real" work.

What's Wrong?

- You'll spill gravy on your documents.
- You're being walked on.
- Your boss is a turkey.
- He's gobbling up your personal time.
- He's taking advantage of his position.
- Soon you'll become his personal masseuse.

Some Success Strategies:

Learn to talk assertively. Express your feelings openly and honestly to coworkers that are demanding too much from you. Stand up for your rights! Tell him your religion doesn't allow you to work on holidays. Refuse to work extra hours that you don't get compensated for. Revisit your job functions and duties with him thoroughly. Politely decline to run his personal errands, and document the dates and times of your request. If the behavior continues, go to a higher authority.

#31 The Yankee Doodler

Your idea of effective office communication is writing illegible comments on notepad paper and leaving them at someone's desk. If you can read it, why can't they?

What's Wrong?

- They can't read it.
- They can't even figure out who wrote it.
- It looks like hieroglyphics.
- Trying to decipher it wastes everyone's time.
- In your case, the sword is mightier than the pen.

Some Success Strategies:

If you have poor handwriting skills, try to type more often—especially when it's a lengthy message. If you're not much of a typist, practice writing a little more carefully. Ask others if they can read your writing better in print or script, and adjust accordingly. Experiment holding your pen at different angles. For short memos, sign your name at the bottom legibly, and write the date and time at the top. Consider communicating in person or via phone more frequently.

#32 You've Got Mail!

It seems that whenever you finish reading all your e-mails, there's a whole batch of new ones in your mailbox. You often fantasize about deleting them all with a click of the mouse, but you know they contain information you need.

What's Wrong?

:(It seems like your whole day is spent sending and receiving messages.

:(You're living in the age of information overload.

:(Getting e-mails used to be fun, but now you hate it.

:(It's jeopardizing your sanity.

:(And you thought the e-mail system was supposed to make your life easier.

Some Success Strategies:

Unless you're waiting for an important e-mail, don't feel obligated to read messages as soon as they arrive. Set aside a particular time of day to deal with them all at once. Read it, respond if necessary, and delete it or file it. Be sure all e-mails you send out are clear and easy to follow. This will help reduce the number of responses. Stick to one topic per e-mail, and keep the message brief. Correspondents will tend to write brief responses back. Use "unless I/you hear" and "please respond by" within your messages to control the flow of information.

#33 Speaking Your Mind

It's annoying when people interrupt while you're interrupting. Basically you love hearing yourself talk. However, you've noticed that people have stopped glancing at their watches—they're looking at their calendars instead.

What's Wrong?

- Others hide from you when they can.
- You're annoying and giving others headaches.
- It's inconsiderate of those trying to work.
- The wise man listens, and you know the rest.
- They often fight over you. (The loser has to sit next to you.)

Some Success Strategies:

Think before opening your mouth and don't say something without an overall purpose. Don't dominate discussions. Actively listen to those who are speaking to you and practice using nonverbal communication techniques (i.e., nodding, smiling, etc.). Ask open-ended questions to allow listeners the chance to talk. Keep unproductive socializing to a minimum. Lay off the coffee for awhile.

#34 Skeletons In The Closet

You're very open with your personal life at work, and derive pleasure from sharing intimate details of your amorous weekend adventures with your work buddies.

What's Wrong?

- Anything you say may be used against you.
- You're an inspiration for office gossip.
- Others might not care to hear about it.
- You may be perceived as a braggart.
- Don't be surprised to find your stories in the local tabloids.

Some Success Strategies:

Avoid giving away details about your life outside of work that may damage your reputation. Assume that anything you talk about in front of coworkers, either during work or outside of work, can be used to someone else's advantage. Remember that mixing business with friendships is not always a good idea. Before revealing personal secrets, consider the consequences if the word gets around!

Chapter 4

Behavioral Blunders

#35 Pound For Pound

When things don't work right, you take your aggressions out by tearing reports, throwing pens, and smashing your keyboard.

What's Wrong?

- You don't respect company property.
- It only makes the situation worse.
- You're costing the company in repairs.
- You belong in a cage.
- Inanimate objects don't learn by abuse.
- Keep it up, and you'll be making a living selling furniture—your own.

Some Success Strategies:

Remain professional when handling frustrating situations, and think before acting out your aggressions. Try to eliminate problems once and for all by solving them right the first time. Acknowledge your feelings without losing self-control, and apologize when you lose your temper in front of others. If the problems appear overwhelming, enlist the help of others. You don't have to face your troubles alone.

#36 Hey, I Just Work Here!

You've probably heard it a thousand times before: "The customer is always right." You may even believe it. However, whenever an irate customer raises her voice at you, you yell right back.

What's Wrong?

- 📣 They might not do business with your company again.
- 📣 You need an attitude adjustment.
- 📣 Without customers, you wouldn't have a job.
- 📣 You're spreading a negative image of yourself and the organization.
- 📣 Someone will eventually file a complaint against you.
- 📣 You're definitely not a people person.

Some Success Strategies:

Always be courteous when working with your company's customers and vendors. When dealing with a difficult customer, talk in a soft, friendly tone. Don't escalate the situation by arguing. Kill them with kindness. Take a course on effective customer service. Actively solicit and effectively handle customer feedback, complaints, and problems. If you have a short temper, have someone else handle those *stupid* customers.

#37 Temper, Temper

You have volatile emotions. Sometimes you remain in control, but other times you just want to explode. The big boss is keeping her door locked throughout the day "just in case."

What's Wrong?

- You look disheveled.
- It's no fun being a disgruntled employee.
- You're unstable.
- Everyone's frightened of you.
- They avoid you at all costs.
- Management is installing a metal detector in the lobby.

Some Success Strategies:

Channel your anger into constructive tasks. Try exercising or getting involved in hobbies. Avoid displaying hostile feelings, and try to remain calm and poised. When angry, slowly count backwards from ten to one, and take deep breaths often. Keep your voice even in tone and moderation. Write your thoughts down on paper, and share your frustrations with those who have an empathetic ear.

#38 Got Any Change?

You're often reluctant to change things that have worked in the past. You always do what you've always done, so you always get what you've always got.

What's Wrong?

- You're viewed as stubborn.
- Doing the same thing all the time is boring.
- Learning is diminished.
- You may be missing opportunities to improve current processes.
- The competition will pass you by.
- You remain stagnant.

Some Success Strategies:

When one of "your processes" is changed, don't treat it as a personal attack. Always look for new and innovative alternative ways of doing things. Treat the future in terms of what "can be," not what "has been." Recognize the past as a foundation that got you where you are today. Adapt to the ever-changing needs of your organization and its clients by becoming a supporter of continuous process improvement. Question current systems, policies, and procedures to seek enhancements.

#39 Doubting Thomas

You're very cynical about the future of the company you work for, and go out of your way to express your thoughts to anyone who will listen. If you get enough followers, maybe you can start a revolution.

What's Wrong?

- Being a pessimist is your choice, but asking others to "join the dark side" is going overboard.
- Depression is contagious.
- You're hurting company moral.
- No one wants to work with you.
- Others tune you out.
- If you expect the worst, that's what you'll experience.

Some Success Strategies:

Don't wallow in discontent. Look at the positives your company has achieved, and keep them fresh in your mind. Ask to see your company's vision, mission, and long-term objectives. Keep a list of your personal and departmental accomplishments and refer to it when you feel skeptical. Partner with positive people who express enthusiasm. Avoid asking "why" questions, and instead focus on "how" and "when." It's your duty to be supportive and respectful of your company. If you can't be, then leave.

#40 Another Monday...
Oh Joy!

Your job has become increasingly dull. The only thing you look forward to is payday and the weekends. Besides, how else will you pay your bills?

What's Wrong?

✖ You belittled your self-worth.

✖ Maybe you're in the wrong field of work.

✖ Money isn't everything.

✖ You're work is becoming increasingly tedious, boring, and slow.

✖ It just isn't funny.

Some Success Strategies:

Look for the fun in what you do, and try to enjoy your work. Find out what interests you in your position and try to do more of it. Maybe you just need to act enthusiastic. Eventually, you'll feel that way! If that doesn't work, request to take on new and challenging tasks. Perhaps you need some time off to think things over and get away from it all. Consider transferring to another division or department. Still unhappy? Quit while you're ahead.

#41 The Unhappy Camper

Your supervisor gave you another *stupid* task! You return to your desk grumbling, complaining, and hating life.

What's Wrong?

- You're openly demonstrating a lack of interest in your job.
- Whining and resentment will lead to your demise.
- Once others hear you griping, they'll be reluctant to join in on the project.
- Time goes by slower when you're doing something you don't want to do.
- Work is not always fun.
- Besides, why do you think they call it "work"?

Some Success Strategies:

Be agreeable and willing to go the extra mile on tasks that seem tedious or unimportant to you. You'll be remembered for your dedication and efforts. Don't always try to work on the "star" projects, and remember that it's the little things that count. Try to create enthusiasm about getting the task completed successfully and efficiently. At least be grateful you're still employed!

#42 Are We Having Fun Yet?

You really love your work! Who wouldn't if their hours were spent making gadgets out of office supplies and frolicking with coworkers? When your manager walks by, you ingeniously pretend to be hard at work.

What's Wrong?

- Overburdened coworkers will report you.
- Management will soon catch on to your act.
- You're displaying poor work ethics.
- Play-time privileges will be taken away.
- It's immature.
- You'll eventually be transferred to the company's day care center.

Some Success Strategies:

Place the well-being of your organization ahead of your own desire for entertainment. Discover your objectives and work towards achieving them. Remember that job satisfaction comes from being a consistent performer, so develop expertise in what you do and look for your direct contribution to the organization as a whole. Clarify your job description and performance expectations with your manager.

#43 Be Like Me

You simply don't get along with others who don't think, act, and behave like you do. You believe your way is always the correct way.

What's Wrong?

☞ What works for you doesn't work for everybody.

☞ You're isolating yourself.

☞ Disregarding individual diversity blocks learning and new ideas.

☞ Cloning isn't for humans yet.

☞ No two people are alike—and everyone who knows *you* is glad of it.

Some Success Strategies:

Accept the fact that everyone is different! Respect all forms of diversity including race, gender, culture, and religion. View each coworker as being equally valuable to the organization, and try to capitalize on diverse team members' strengths. Don't be judgemental or base your perceptions on first impressions. Work together on mutual goals to keep yourself focused on results, not differences. You'll be surprised at how much you really do have in common.

#44 Wake-Up Calls

You're having a spirited debate with a coworker over the telephone when suddenly you get another call. Without realizing it, you answer the phone shouting, "What do you want?!"

What's Wrong?

- The caller isn't sure who they're talking to.
- The introduction sets the overall mood of the conversation.
- You give the impression you're not interested in what they have to say.
- You sound too busy to talk.
- This is not creating rapport.
- It could be your CEO on the other end.

Some Success Strategies:

Don't take your aggressions out on an innocent caller, or anyone else for that matter. Your facial expressions and emotions can be conveyed through your voice. In between phone calls, separate yourself emotionally and physically before picking up. Relax, smile, and take a deep breath. Then, answer the call with the proper company/departmental greeting.

#45 5:00? I'm Outta Here!

When your work shift ends, you drop whatever you're doing and promptly leave—even during emergencies and staff meetings. Hey, if they paid you a little more, maybe you'd feel obligated to stick around a little longer.

What's Wrong?

- You aren't dedicated to your job.
- It causes havoc during business emergencies.
- You haven't dropped the high school mentality.
- You'll just end up in rush-hour traffic anyway.
- Time goes by slower when you're clock-watching.
- It's inconsiderate.

Some Success Strategies:

If there's a problem that can't be resolved during your regular shift, don't leave without telling someone about it. If you can't stay overtime to help out, consider calling the office when you get home to ask if everything's under control. Bosses love that kind of stuff. Even if it's just a typical day, it's always a good idea to inform your supervisor before you leave. Otherwise, you might find the infamous message on your desk in the morning: "Please see me as soon as you get in."

Chapter 5

Habitual Habits

#46 Ill-Fated

Your sick days always seem to be planned around weekends and holidays. When you come back to work with a tan, you simply explain that the sun helps dry out your sinuses.

What's Wrong?

- Your credibility is shot.
- Being "out sick" creates an extra burden on others.
- If asked for a doctor's note upon your return, you'll have to forge one.
- You fall behind on projects.
- You'll be out of sick days when you really need them.
- You could get skin cancer.

Some Success Strategies:

Don't abuse your sick days. Consider the implications on others by not showing up. Be honest and ask for personal time off. Use vacation days if you have any left. If you're really too sick to come in, notify your supervisor before the work day begins or as soon as reasonably possible. And while you're on the phone, make occasional sniffling noises and talk while squeezing your nostrils together to create that special "congested head effect."

#47 Garbage In, Garbage Out

When you submit forms, they're often halfway filled out, or completely blank. Oral communication is your preferred mode of communication, and you intend to keep it that way.

What's Wrong?

- Typically, forms exist for a reason.
- You lack attention to detail.
- You make others hunt down missing information.
- The records are invalid.
- Others are forced to act on hunches.
- You have no backup record of your actions.

Some Success Strategies:

Don't pass on work in a form in which you wouldn't want to receive it. Adhere to the established guidelines and rules of the organization. If you don't understand the correct procedures, ask those who do. Request that the forms be made shorter and easier to fill out, and see if some of them can be automated or eliminated all together. Though you may be obligated to utilize the forms, it's also your duty to provide suggestions for improvement.

#48 Putting Off Today What You Can Do Tomorrow

Most of your work day is spent in crisis management and fire-fighting. The fact is, if it weren't for the last minute, you wouldn't get any work done at all.

What's Wrong?

- There's a simple word for it—procrastination.
- Unnecessary stress is placed on yourself and others.
- Everyone is operating in panic mode.
- Chances for errors increase.
- You're unnecessarily being billed for rush jobs.
- Eventually you'll miss a major deadline.

Some Success Strategies:

Don't wait until the last minute to do something you could have done a long time ago. Always allow time for up-front planning before beginning projects. Use your time wisely! Try to anticipate potential obstacles before they become a reality. Keep your calendar up-to-date, and analyze deadlines and milestones on a regular basis. If there seems to be more work to do than time available to do it, solicit the help of your colleagues or manager.

#49 If You Snooze, You Lose

You have a track record of being late for work. Your car was towed, the power went out, and one day your kids hid your car keys. People are placing bets on what you'll come up with next.

What's Wrong?

- You're setting a bad example.
- People can't locate you during morning emergencies.
- You're unreliable and losing respect.
- You're missing out.
- You might get fired.
- All the donuts will be gone by the time you stroll into the office.

Some Success Strategies:

Be honest with yourself and find the "true root" cause of what's making you late, and take steps to eliminate or reduce it. If getting up is the problem, arrange for a "phone buddy" to call you in the morning, or buy an automatic coffee maker. If TV shows keep you up late, record them for later viewing. Traffic? Check traffic reports regularly, and consider carpooling, leaving earlier, or moving closer to work. Ask your supervisor about alternative work hours.

#50 Clearance Denied

You often make important decisions without notifying management. Your philosophy of eliminating the middle man is making your supervisor a little nervous.

What's Wrong?

- You're power hungry.

- You appear disrespectful of your supervisor's inputs and decisions.

- He'll start thinking of ways to deny your clearance.

- You'll be responsible for any mishaps.

- The line will be drawn when you start parking your car in the boss's parking space.

Some Success Strategies:

Clarify where your responsibility starts and stops, and how it fits with that of others. Go through the proper chain of command. If appropriate decision-makers are unavailable, get the go-ahead from upper management before making decisions that you aren't authorized to make. If you are a member of an empowered team that can make their own decisions, always consult the other team members first before taking action.

#51 Paperboy

Your paperwork is typically strewn all over the place. It often takes you hours to find things. Sometimes you can't stand it anymore, so you go work at someone else's desk, and make a mess there as well.

What's Wrong?

- You appear disorganized and scatterbrained.
- You're setting a poor example for others.
- Important documents are misplaced.
- A tremendous amount of time is wasted searching for things.
- Incoming paperwork is lost in the shuffle.
- Your workstation is considered a fire hazard.

Some Success Strategies:

Take a class on organization. Develop a simple, yet effective filing system. Try to handle each piece of paper only once, and tackle the highest priority items first. Computerize paperwork whenever possible, and avoid printing e-mails and documents that you can read online. Don't stockpile papers you will never read. Throw it away! Get off unnecessary distribution and mailing lists. Ask for more storage areas. Get in the habit of cleaning and organizing your desk at the end of each day.

#52 I Wanna Hold Your Hand

You're often waiting for someone else to tell you what to do, when to do it, and how to do it. By not taking responsibility, you can never be blamed for anything that might go wrong.

What's Wrong?

- Your focus is narrow.
- You're not displaying any initiative.
- Constant hand-holding slows others down.
- You're not considered promotional material.
- You don't trust your own judgment.
- When others tell you that your mother dresses you funny, they're being serious.

Some Success Strategies:

Take initiative, and constantly strive to find new and better ways to perform tasks. Always be willing to accept new and challenging projects. Look for work that needs to be done, and request to take total responsibility for tasks that you now only do a part of. Work towards becoming autonomous, and don't be afraid of failure. Move out of your mother's house and get your own apartment.

#53 Behind The Times

You're comfortable working with the same old office equipment you've used for years. Besides, you can't find the time to catch up with the newer technologies. You stick with the old fashioned methods of doing business until forced otherwise.

What's Wrong?

- You'll become obsolete.

- You're not taking advantage of modern equipment that can increase your productivity.

- The office lingo confuses you.

- You're giving the impression that you don't care about your future.

- Everyone laughed at the last office party when you tried to fit your 45's into the CD player.

Some Success Strategies:

Commit yourself to being a lifetime learner. Use technologies first to accomplish familiar tasks, then branch out. Keep up-to-date with technical skills relevant to the job and business trends. Read trade journals and magazines related to your field. Utilize your company's available learning resources (books, computer-based training, videos, tutorials, the Internet, etc.). Attend company-paid seminars and training sessions whenever possible.

#54 Well . . . I Forget

You've just remembered something your boss asked you to do a month ago. The deadline has already passed. There's nothing left to do but pray she forgot about it too.

What's Wrong?

- Forgetfulness is a sign of senility.
- You'll be constantly worrying about it.
- If you hold out any longer, things will just get worse.
- She will remember it sooner or later.
- You'll be the only employee with three baskets on your desk (in, out, and oops).

Some Success Strategies:

If you've forgotten to do a request, don't make excuses. Explain to your supervisor that you've simply made a mistake, and offer suggestions on how the situation can be avoided in the future. Focus on getting the problem solved. Next time, avoid multi-tasking to the point where your attention is diverted. Don't try to keep things in your head. Create a master to-do list, and when given a new task, write it down before you forget.

#55 Analysis-Paralysis

You have a hard time making decisions and require all the facts before deciding how to tackle a new project. Even then, you fear making the wrong choice, so you decide to analyze the situation a little longer.

What's Wrong?

- Projects remain on hold.
- Procrastination can make a decision more difficult to make.
- They'll always give you simple, no-brainer tasks.
- You're a bottleneck.
- Delays lessen the time available for corrective action.
- Your personal advisor is the local psychic.

Some Success Strategies:

Learn to accept reasonable risks, and make the best decision with the available facts. Don't allow yourself to go on to a new task until the previous one is finished. Set clear project priorities, deadlines, and checkpoints, and stick to them! If you need to make a quick decision, consider passing the reins over to someone else.

#56 All Work And No Play

You're completely dedicated to your job. You can't understand why others are reluctant to work double shifts or on holidays.

What's Wrong?

- 🚀 It makes you a dull boy.
- 🚀 Your health may suffer.
- 🚀 No one will take you seriously when you're wearing a straight jacket.
- 🚀 Workaholics die young.
- 🚀 It's hard to get a tan from the moon.
- 🚀 Even the janitors feel sorry for you.

Some Success Strategies:

Don't let your work dominate your entire life. Avoid picking up dinner from the office vending machine. Make your physical well-being a number one priority. When you're facing project deadlines, arrange to take extra time off once completed. Regularly and openly review workloads, hours worked, expectations, and priorities with your supervisor.

Chapter 6

Ethical Enigmas

#57 Now You See Me, Now You Don't

Throughout the day, you're able to disappear and reappear without a lot of nosy coworkers asking where you've been. You use this to your advantage to run important errands such as shopping for clothes, having your nails done, seeing matinee movies, and getting a haircut.

What's Wrong?

- You're missing in action.
- The lost time needs to be made up sooner or later.
- You're abusing your position.
- Your priorities need to be adjusted.
- They might change the locks when you're out.

Some Success Strategies:

If you must leave the office to run a personal errand, inform someone where you're going and when you anticipate to be back. Consider borrowing a pager when you're out, and be sure to call someone if you're going to be late returning. Schedule personal appointments around weekends and off-hours whenever possible.

#58 Not Enough Hours In A Day

You feel good about putting in a full day's work ... on your time sheet, that is. By rounding off to the nearest hour, you succeed in expanding six hours into eight. If anyone ever asks about it, you can always say you took a short lunch.

What's Wrong?

- Cutting corners will only hurt you in the long run.

- You're walking on thin ice.

- Lying about hours is subject to termination.

- You're getting too big for your britches.

- Time is of the essence—the essence of your poor performance review.

Some Success Strategies:

If you think you're getting away with something, think again. Always put in your full time while at work—yes, even on Fridays. If your personal life doesn't allow you to work a full shift, consider going part-time or working less hours. If your motive for leaving early is to beat traffic or to pick up your kids, ask your supervisor if you can leave earlier by coming in earlier.

#59 Fringe Benefits

You save yourself both time and money by staying after hours to use your company's resources for personal use. During the holiday season, you use the color printer to create personalized greeting cards and ship them priority next day air.

What's Wrong?

- Using company property for personal reasons is dishonest.
- Believe it or not, someone has to pay for this.
- You might get caught in the act.
- They'll take your keys away.
- You're a freeloader.
- It's time to panic when your resumé gets jammed in the photocopier.

Some Success Strategies:

Gain the trust of others by avoiding misuse of company property. Go to an outside business service for personal photocopies, faxes, and other services during your lunch hour. Many of these businesses are open 24 hours and have laser printing and mailing services as well. Purchase a home computer system.

#60 If At First You Don't Succeed, Pry Pry Again

Your sources of previously confidential information come from listening in on private conversations, reading incoming faxes, and searching trash cans after hours. "Knowledge is power," you tell yourself.

What's Wrong?

- You don't respect the privacy of others.
- You might run across incorrect information—and believe it.
- If caught, you'll lose the trust of everyone.
- You're nosy.
- When you accidentally read your supervisor's paystub, you'll really be upset.

Some Success Strategies:

Don't go poking your nose around in areas not normally accessible to you. When going into an unoccupied office, turn the lights on and make your presence known. If you need specific information to be more productive and make informed job decisions, prepare your case in advance and present it to your supervisor.

#61 Numbers Don't Lie, But Do You?

By swapping a few numbers around and making up a few, you were able to make your project appear to be on time and under budget.

What's Wrong?

- The next quota will be even higher.

- You might be haunted with having to cover up more and more information.

- If caught, you'll lose your credibility.

- Management's strategic efforts are misdirected.

- By covering up the facts, you give no incentive to make things better.

- They consider you the founder of "new math."

Some Success Strategies:

If you're unhappy with your figures, don't manipulate the truth! Analyze why your numbers are the way they are, and take steps to improve them. If your budget was too low to begin with, request that it be increased to an adequate level next time. Inform others ahead of time when your project is going beyond your budget. Accurately plan all time and resources needed before your project begins.

#62 Phone Home

Your lunch hour is the perfect time for making phone calls, so you creatively spread your lunch hour throughout the day. Not only can you call friends and family across the nation, no one ever deducts the charges from your paycheck.

What's Wrong?

- "Freedom of speech" does not apply here.
- You're distracting coworkers.
- You're unproductive and set a bad example.
- Personal phone calls cost organizations millions of dollars.
- Your extension is busy when work-related calls come in.
- Coworkers know who your friends are before you introduce them.

Some Success Strategies:

When you need to make a personal call during business hours, ask for permission first and use an unoccupied office. For long distance calls, use a calling card or charge it back to your home phone number. Be selective in giving out your work number. Maybe get a pager or have the receptionist direct incoming calls from personal acquaintances to your voice mail. If all else fails, consider writing letters or sending e-mails.

#63 Network Opportunities

The company's computer network is full of useful information, and you've become adept at weaving your way through the assortment of gateways and servers. As you stumble across the employee payroll database, you contemplate looking up the CEO's annual salary.

What's Wrong?

- You're playing with fire.
- It's called "hacking."
- Important records may be accidentally altered.
- It's an invasion of privacy.
- You may have already triggered security alarms.
- Curiosity killed the cat.

Some Success Strategies:

Refrain from abusing your security privileges. Don't even attempt to access confidential employee records, especially those of upper management! If you need specific information from someone's computer, ask them for a hardcopy printout or a copy of the file. If you have a business need for confidential information, request that your security access be increased.

#64 Fast Food Take Out

When no one's around, you use the lunchroom refrigerator as a smorgasbord. Your general rule of thumb is, "If it's still there after dark—it's up for grabs."

What's Wrong?

- You're inconsiderate.
- It'll be humiliating if you get caught.
- It's stealing.
- You're not at your parents' house.
- Coworkers go hungry the next day.
- One of these days you'll sink your greedy teeth into a moldy egg salad sandwich.

Some Success Strategies:

Be considerate of others and their personal belongings. If you know something's not yours, then don't take it without asking. Remember to bring a lunch to work, or have another coworker go and get you something. If you're that hungry, consider ordering a pizza or two. Keep a supply of healthy snacks at your desk. If you ever decide to bring your own food, label it with your name, and don't let it turn into a science project.

#65 Sabotaging Success

One of your peers always outperforms you and gets constant recognition from management. You're considering sabotaging her latest assignment to put her in her place.

What's Wrong?

- You're jealous.
- If caught, you could be fired.
- The whole department will suffer.
- It's just plain evil.
- You'll feel guilty afterwards.
- There's no rest for the wicked.
- Maybe you misunderstood the title of this book.

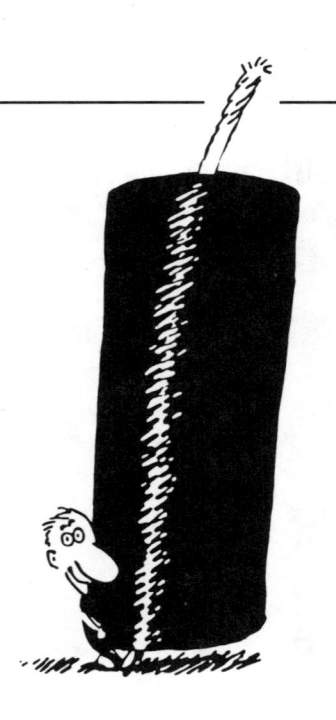

Some Success Strategies:

Don't do it. Remember that success is the best revenge. If someone has stronger abilities than you, challenge yourself to surpass them. Have them become your mentor. Ask for their opinion and advice often. If you simply don't have the stuff, seek other ways to be recognized or consider transferring to another department.

#66 I Know Something You Don't Know

You just love collecting the latest dirt on other employees. Secrets go in one ear and out your mouth.

What's Wrong?

- A faithful employee may expose you as the source of gossip.
- Others start to think you're bad-mouthing them as well.
- Your integrity is shot.
- Telling secrets gives away your personal power.
- Coworkers feel free to share the information with everyone else.
- The information might not be accurate to begin with.

Some Success Strategies:

Be trustworthy with confidential information and the opinions of others shared with you in confidence. Resist the temptation of spreading information that may damage an employee's reputation or that can harm your organization's reputation. Instead, work on spreading positive rumors. Don't listen to others who are gossiping, and defend those being put down by others.

#67 Double-Time

Having gained marketable skills from your present organization, you've been able to do independent consulting for extra income. You don't really consider it a side business, since you can usually get away with conducting it on company time.

What's Wrong?

- Technically, you're getting paid twice.
- It's completely unethical.
- You're greedy.
- You're gambling with your career.
- Your loyalty is divided.
- If exposed, you'll find yourself more independent than you had bargained for.

Some Success Strategies:

There's nothing wrong with having an entrepreneurial attitude, but wait until you're on personal time before you start doing outside work. Adopt your employer's interest as your own while you're on company time. Be sure your side work doesn't cause conflict with your employer's interests. In addition, don't discuss your own business in front of others coworkers or try to recruit them. Avoid giving your work number out to your clients.

Chapter 7

Teamwork Troubles

#68 Don't Test Me!

You overreact and criticize your team members when they make common errors. Sometimes their carelessness drives you insane! If they had only followed your direction, mistakes like these wouldn't occur.

What's Wrong?

☞ You need to lighten up!

☞ Team members only get defensive.

☞ You're annoying.

☞ Everyone will avoid showing their work to you or asking for your opinion.

☞ Nobody's perfect.

☞ When you make a mistake yourself, they'll announce it in the next company newsletter.

Some Success Strategies:

Often times people take criticisms personally. Be tolerant and remember that people grow from mistakes. Advise the person on how to correct the mistake without unjustly dwelling on the error itself. Be aware that some mistakes are caused by a "breakdown" somewhere else down the line, and that it might be uncontrollable. Be willing to listen to their defense. Praise team members for doing things right (or approximately right).

#69 Thank You! Thank You! I'm Here All Week

When the opportunity presented itself, you took credit for an idea that wasn't yours. In such a highly competitive environment, you need every advantage you can get.

What's Wrong?

- If the truth is revealed, you'll be in deep water.
- You lose the respect of your coworkers.
- You're conceited.
- You'll create enemies.
- "Your idea" might turn out to be a flop.
- You've certainly made a name for yourself—and everyone whispers it.

Some Success Strategies:

If you've received a compliment on an idea that wasn't yours to begin with, let them know about it! Enhance your image by giving credit to those who deserve it. You'll foster stronger relationships with your peers if they can trust you. Try to create win-win situations for both of you. After all, the credit may mean much more to the other person than it does to you.

#70 Teams Are For Sports

Just hearing the word "teamwork" makes you cringe. You believe it is a bunch of hype. Why should others get any credit for your hard work and efforts?

What's Wrong?

- You're a loner.//
- No one helps you when you need it.
- It's hard to succeed by yourself.
- You're not taking advantage of the power of teamwork.
- Your inflated ego is getting in the way of your success.

Some Success Strategies:

Learn the value and benefits of working with others. Drop the "I'll do it all myself" attitude, and ask for help from other team members when needed. Look for the fun in teamwork! Show a positive attitude, outlook, and morale. Participate in the creation of a shared team purpose and direction. Actively volunteer for assignments in team meetings, and partner with those who have an interest in the team's success and well-being.

#71 Not Another Meeting!

You can't stand meetings. To make matters worse, your team meets at least once a week. For the most part, you just sit there, gazing into nothingness.

What's Wrong?

- Opportunities to share knowledge are being missed.
- You're lost in space.
- You have no idea where your team is headed.
- You'll focus on "important" projects that are not directed toward team objectives.
- You're bored out of your mind.
- Team members have to bring you back to Earth first before they can ask for your input.

Some Success Strategies:

Keep apprised of what others are doing in your department by paying full attention and taking notes during team meetings. Actively participate whenever possible by vocalizing knowledge, providing input, and asking questions. Everyone plays a part in the success of a meeting, so do everything and anything to contribute—regardless of your role. What are the meeting objectives? Work towards achieving them so your meetings are efficient and effective!

#72 What A Concept!

You're quick on the draw to shoot down the new ideas of team members during meetings. Some of your favorite phrases include "Yeah right," "They'll never buy that," and "We've tried that before and look where it got us."

What's Wrong?

- People stop sharing their ideas.
- New concepts and innovations remain untapped.
- Others won't care what you have to say, either.
- The meeting becomes confrontational.
- Creativity suffers.
- You probably don't own a pet rock or a hula-hoop either.

Some Success Strategies:

Unusual ideas are often proven extremely useful! Don't berate unconventional thoughts. Rather, create a team environment with no restrictions on ideas. Respond with interest and an open mind to what your team members say. When faced with common problems, always strive to look for new potential solutions. Don't pass judgment on any viewpoint until all sides of the issue are taken into consideration.

#73 Let Them Eat Cake

When your organization sponsors special parties and events, you rarely show your face. Frankly, you'd prefer it if they spent the money on bonuses instead.

What's Wrong?

- No one comes to your parties either.
- You're not the "company man" they thought you were.
- You look uncommitted and uninterested in your coworkers.
- Money isn't everything.
- You're missing opportunities to mingle with management.
- You're a party-pooper.

Some Success Strategies:

Whenever possible, attend company-sponsored celebrations and events. Such efforts show you have a genuine interest in your fellow coworkers, which creates new opportunities for bonding. Who knows? You may get to see your team members in a different light! Always take time out to celebrate successes—both yours and your coworkers'.

#74 Does He Still Work Here?

You're known as a miracle worker—it's a miracle when you come to work. You'd rather spend your days at home relaxing by the pool, wondering what your team members are doing.

What's Wrong?

- Your dependability takes a nose-dive.
- Others have to work overtime to pick up your slack.
- Absenteeism is a curable disease.
- This is not telecommuting.
- Everyone is forced to work around your schedule.
- Cobwebs are forming at your desk.

Some Success Strategies:

Always consider the impact on others before deciding not to come into work. Strive to maintain an excellent attendance record. Have personal and vacation days pre-approved by your supervisor well in advance. If an unexpected emergency has come up that requires time off, personally notify your supervisor as soon as possible—don't leave it up to another coworker to do your dirty work.

#75 Now Drop And Give Me Twenty!

You've recently been promoted to department team leader. For the first time in your life, you get to tell others what to do. You've already begun to threaten team members with their jobs if they don't follow your orders.

What's Wrong?

- Power has gone to your head.
- You have an unrealistic expectation of others.
- You're unliked by your new subordinates.
- A request usually works better than an order.
- Eventually, they'll overthrow the dictator.

Some Success Strategies:

For starters, you need to learn to talk assertively, not aggressively. Present your requests softly, calmly, and non-threateningly. Don't assert your new authority all at once. Never forget about the people who helped you climb the ladder of success! Gain the respect of your team members by providing them with choices and opportunities to make their own decisions. Work with your team in creating a shared vision and team goals. Attend a course in leadership or effective management.

#76 Absolutely, 100%, Not Guilty

You want everyone to think you're perfect. When you make a mistake, you try to weasel your way out of it by blaming it on erroneous work processes, poor policies, and innocent bystanders.

What's Wrong?

- You show how insecure you really feel.
- Blaming creates resentment.
- That halo should be a noose.
- You're not resolving the issue at hand.
- You're afraid of taking risks.
- No one expects you to be able to walk on water.

Some Success Strategies:

Be willing to admit your own faults. Don't use a scapegoat when you are equally responsible. Identify what caused you to make that rare mistake, and look for the lesson to be learned. Focus on the solution rather than the problem. Prevent future mistakes by using experience to guide you, and before making rash decisions think through all the ramifications.

#77 Vows Of Silence

You've had a falling out with one of your team members over something really *stupid*, and now the two of you aren't speaking to one another. You're starting to think of devious ways to get her kicked off the team.

What's Wrong?

- She's not going anywhere.
- Dwelling on it will just make you more angry.
- You're not a team player.
- Too much tension may cause you to forfeit your position.
- The progress of your team is penalized.
- Communication is blocked.
- It's silly.

Some Success Strategies:

If you experience personal conflict with one of your team members, don't talk to others about it—tell the person directly! Don't assume things will fix themselves. Take the initiative to find a resolution before issues become emotionally entrenched. Start up conversations again with small talk. Then, try to uncover the underlying causes of the conflict. Is it over role ambiguity? Incompatible working styles? Jealousy? Once you know the core issues, explore ways to resolve the conflict together. Get over it!

#78 No Assistance

You are easily offended when a team member asks you for help on one of his projects. You believe if he can't finish it by himself, he should never have taken on the assignment in the first place.

What's Wrong?

☞ It appears to others that you don't care about the overall success of your team.

☞ You're missing opportunities to "save the day."

☞ You're acting selfishly.

☞ It fosters resentment.

☞ You have a bad attitude.

☞ No one will lift a finger when *you* need it.

Some Success Strategies:

Act in the best interest of your team rather than yourself. Learn to work *with* team members, not *against* them. Be willing to go the extra mile in assisting team members with projects that are important to them. However, if you are working on a project that you feel has a higher priority or is more important, ask your supervisor first before switching your focus.

Chapter 8
Management Mishaps

#79 On A Need-To-Know Basis

Your supervisor asked you to proof a presentation that she's giving to senior management. You noticed a lot of it was wrong, and there were even typos. You decided not to say anything about it to make her look *stupid*.

What's Wrong?

- It's egotistical and immature.
- You're intentionally creating chaos.
- There's definitely a communication problem.
- She'll feel betrayed.
- The ultimate blame will fall upon you.
- She'll stop telling you when your zipper's down.

Some Success Strategies:

Don't withhold important and relevant information. Avoid complicating your boss's job! You were hired to help out, not to make things more difficult. Direct your attention to helping your boss achieve her goals by going beyond your ordinary job functions. Teach your boss how things are done.

#80 Out Of Sight, Out Of Mind

You've been working behind the scenes and making things happen—for other people. You'd probably have a great reputation around the office if they really knew who did all the work. Even your supervisor has a hard time recalling your name.

What's Wrong?

- You're an unknown entity.
- Chances for a deserved promotion are minimal.
- You have no authority.
- You're a prime target during layoffs.
- You feel taken advantage of.
- You're never in the limelight.

Some Success Strategies:

Increase your visibility by working on special projects for executives. Volunteer for internal committees and associations. Try to increase contact with powerful people or people who are close to powerful people. Extend a visible presence at key social gatherings and events. Get your name on distribution lists that have powerful people listed. Don't be modest about your successful accomplishments.

#81 What Do You Mean I Can't Take Criticism?!

During your last performance review, the boss mentioned that you couldn't take criticism very well. You thought his comments were totally out of line, and you proceeded to spew out an assortment of finger-pointing comments, back talk, and rationalizations.

What's Wrong?

- You just proved his point.
- You're not taking responsibility for your own behavior.
- Being overly defensive is a sign of weakness.
- You're demonstrating a total lack of professionalism.
- This is how arguments start.
- You're not making your boss' job any easier.

Some Success Strategies:

Receive and act on constructive feedback non-defensively. Try not to take feedback as a personal attack, but as an opportunity to improve. Avoid comparing your work to the work of others. Recognize and accommodate for your own limitations. Agree with any valid criticism, and openly discuss ways to improve your behavior and its impacts and consequences on others.

#82 Promotional Material

You've been at your company for many years and have excelled in your current position. However, over the last few years your talents and skills have gone by unnoticed. You believe you're ready for a supervisory role, but your popularity could use a little assistance.

What's Wrong?

- You're not getting the recognition you deserve.
- You're always being overlooked.
- Now is not the time to be humble.
- They'll promote someone who can talk his way into the position.
- You're not assertive enough.

Some Success Strategies:

Offer constructive suggestions that show initiative. Try to identify a pressing organizational problem, find a solution that will result in high visibility, and implement the solution competently and successfully. Author critical memos and reports. Vocalize your subject matter expertise in meetings. Post diplomas, certificates, and licenses. Speak with authority. Write an article for the company newsletter.

#83 So, How's Life At The Top?

You're very casual when speaking with upper management, asking personal questions, addressing them as "buddies" or "pals," and inviting them over to your place for dinner.

What's Wrong?

- They may think you want something from them, or that you have ulterior motives.
- Being overly casual may be viewed as being disrespectful.
- It may make some people uncomfortable.
- You're being too friendly.
- It's inappropriate.

Some Success Strategies:

Don't assume a familiarity that has not been established, especially when doing business with those from other cultures and backgrounds. Develop relationships formally at first, then work towards informality. Show respect for others by actively listening when spoken to, valuing their judgment, and following proper etiquette. Pay attention to how others successfully interact with management and follow their lead.

#84 You've Disrespected The Family

You've always been a firm believer in love at first sight. In short, it saves a lot of time. At the last company picnic, you tried to land a few good-bye kisses from some of the managers' spouses before leaving.

What's Wrong?

- Only desperate people would attempt this.
- If you're trying to kiss up to your boss, you have bad aim.
- Your grandkids will always ask you to retell the story of how you lost your teeth.
- You have poor morals.
- It destroys marriages.
- Loose lips sink ships.

Some Success Strategies:

This kind of lip service will only land you in hot water. Refrain from mixing pleasure with other people's business. Use proper greeting and departure etiquette when acquainting yourself with family and guests of your fellow workers. Ask your colleagues if they know someone outside of the organization they could set you up with (single, of course). Adopt a pet to keep you company at home.

#85 The Boss's Pet

You're under the impression that laughing heartily at your boss's *stupid* jokes and agreeing with everything she says will get you a large bonus.

What's Wrong?

☺ If your boss wanted a yes-man, she would have hired one.

☺ She may think you're trying to cover up for a lack of competence.

☺ You're not fooling anyone.

☺ Your peers think you're deceptive.

☺ What your boss says isn't always funny.

☺ Your bonus will be a new flea collar.

Some Success Strategies:

It's okay to play some of these little political games once in awhile, but don't overdo it. Avoid being overly pleasing, nice, or agreeable just for the sake of trying to make others like you. Don't purposefully park next to their cars, stay extra hours because of their presence, or follow them around the office. Learn to disagree once in awhile! You might open up a new perspective on how things are done.

#86 Speak Now, Or Forever Hold Your Peace

You have a few good suggestions on how things should be done around the office, but presenting your ideas to management makes you very uncomfortable.

What's Wrong?

- Whenever they're around, you start sweating profusely.
- You're so nervous that your words come out jumbled.
- Your suggestions will never be implemented.
- Someone else will take credit for your ideas.
- You're also the type of person who makes *stupid* mistakes only when they're watching.

Some Success Strategies:

Relax! Executives are human too. Treat them as equals—don't unnecessarily magnify them. Spend more time around them and get to know them. Then, comfortably and openly voice your thoughts, feelings, and suggestions—even if your ideas conflict with others, or are not widely shared. Present your ideas as options, not as definite solutions. Practice your presentation on a coworker.

#87 Head Over Heels

You and your boss have always enjoyed working closely together, but recently you've been getting just a little too close. You've already reserved two airline tickets for a special business trip to Paris.

What's Wrong?

♥ You're looking for love in all the wrong places.

♥ Coworkers will claim you're getting preferential treatment.

♥ Roles get confused.

♥ Your boss will have to add another category onto your performance review.

♥ It's awkward.

♥ If things don't work out, you may end up divorcing your job.

Some Success Strategies:

Dating your boss is considered an organizational taboo. If you think otherwise, maybe you're just too love-struck to see it. Separate your work from your love life. Work on developing relationships outside of work instead. Focus on maintaining a friendship with your boss instead of a courtship. Transfer to another division or department if you wish to continue the relationship.

#88 Power To The People!

You intentionally keep your supervisor in the dark about the status of your work in order to remain in control of decisions and keep the upper hand. Management is virtually clueless as to what you do all day.

What's Wrong?

- Without your supervisor's input, you could make incorrect decisions.
- You'll get blamed if things go wrong.
- No one really knows what you're doing or how long it takes.
- Your supervisor may be suspicious of being manipulated.
- Important deadlines may be missed.
- You're considering joining Anarchists Anonymous.

Some Success Strategies:

Always be willing to share job-related information to those who need it. Learn to respect your supervisor's input and advice, and develop open lines of communication by regularly communicating project updates. Create a calendar containing important milestones and deadlines, and make it accessible to others. Keep key players apprised of all important challenges, successes, and delays.

#89 Party Fowls

You wake up with a hangover. Your underwear is missing. You have a black eye. You're in jail. Last night was the office Christmas party.

What's Wrong?

- You made a fool of yourself.
- Coworkers will never forget about it.
- You missed out on all the fun.
- Even the legal department won't bail you out.
- You won't be released from jail until after the holidays.
- They've already taken your name off the company phone list.

Some Success Strategies:

Nothing's wrong with having a little fun at company parties and events, but don't go overboard. Remember where you are! Try to act refined and somewhat level-headed, especially when you're around those who sign your paycheck. Engage yourself with conversations, games, and other activities instead of over-indulging yourself beyond coherency. Don't always try to be the life of the party. Bring someone with you who can control you. Consider leaving early.

Chapter 9

Simply Stupid

#90 The Sound Of Music

Your favorite office music is broadcasted by the local rock and roll radio station. As you crank the volume up another level, you begin to wonder if your boss can hear it from across the hall.

What's Wrong?

♪ Coworkers can't concentrate on their work.

♪ They might not appreciate your taste in music.

♪ Others have to compete for air space by talking louder.

♪ Concerts are for weekends.

♪ It creates an atmosphere unconducive for business.

♪ Something's definitely wrong when coworkers start bringing earplugs to work.

Some Success Strategies:

Bringing personal radios to work is a common novelty, however, always be courteous to others trying to work or talk on the phone. Keep the volume low or shut it off entirely. Don't play music at a level that causes distractions or prevents you or others from being productive. Consider switching to easy-listening music. If you really can't stand the silence, wear a headset. Above all, don't sing along—especially if you don't know the words.

#91 Suitability

You always dress your best when you come to work, but the only problem is that you have just one best dress.

What's Wrong?

- You look cheap.
- It looks like you don't care about your appearance.
- There's speculation if you ever went home.
- It's unoriginal and boring.
- Your coworkers wonder when (or if) you ever wash your clothes.
- You have no style.
- Others laugh behind your back.

Some Success Strategies:

Don't wait until your birthday for new clothes. Shop at discount clothing stores and buy outfits that you can mix and match. Change your clothing accessories often (i.e., vests, jackets, skirts, belts, ties, scarves, shoes, etc.). Try not to wear the same thing twice in one week. Give outdated clothing to the needy.

#92 Fashionably Late

You're chronically late for staff meetings due to more pressing issues. When you finally do arrive, everyone stops talking and stares at you until you take your seat.

What's Wrong?

- ⌛ It's embarrassing.
- ⌛ They've started without you.
- ⌛ It looks like you don't respect the time of others.
- ⌛ Important details are missed.
- ⌛ Everyone's time is wasted bringing you up to speed.
- ⌛ It's disruptive and irritating.
- ⌛ Others will think they can get away with it as well.

Some Success Strategies:

Be punctual with meetings and other commitments. Arrive early if you have to. Know the purpose of the meeting beforehand so you can come prepared. If an unexpected emergency has come up that forces you to be late, notify the attendees in advance so they can either reschedule or arrange to give you a copy of the meeting minutes. Consider listening in on the meeting through a speakerphone or intercom while you sit at your desk.

#93 Quick And Dirty

Over the years, you've become a master of solving problems for the time being. You're content as long as you can get it working again the fastest way possible.

What's Wrong?

- You're lazy.
- You may be making the problem worse.
- You're not digging deep enough to uncover the source of the problem.
- By not fixing the "true root" cause, you're allowing the problem to resurface time after time.
- Shortcuts are often unwise and may ultimately cost more time and money.

Some Success Strategies:

Don't make critical decisions before all the necessary facts are in. Use brainstorming or other problem-solving techniques to find the root cause of the problem. Then, take steps to eliminate it. Remember, if you don't have time to do it right, when will you have time to do it over? Analyze the alternatives. Come up with several solutions to the problem, and get the opinions of others when appropriate.

#94 Hook, Line, And Sinker

You've been secretly dating someone from your office, but your cover was almost blown when a few coworkers saw the two of you having dinner together. You fed them an impromptu line about having a business meeting.

What's Wrong?

- They'll jokingly accuse you of "fishing off the company pier."

- Something's a little fishy when you start coming into work together.

- When people start comparing notes, you'll have more problems to tackle.

- Everyone clams up when you enter the lunchroom.

Some Success Strategies:

If you're involved in an office romance and wish to continue it, keep it discreet. Don't let the relationship affect your productivity. Limit phone calls to each other, and discuss personal matters outside of the office. Avoid giving public exhibitions such as playing footsies during meetings, conducting romantic interludes in the hallways, e-mailing love notes, etc. Act professionally around each other. Save your romantic encounters for after hours (and that doesn't mean in the copy room).

#95 Hostel Takeovers

You were working awfully late last night and didn't feel like driving home. You decided to save yourself a trip by spending the night on the president's leather couch.

What's Wrong?

- You're not prepared for a sleep-over.
- The office is not a hotel.
- You may be violating city ordinances.
- It isn't very safe.
- Your back will hurt the next day.
- The president might come in early and see you in your cute pajamas.

Some Success Strategies:

Prevention is the key here. Don't work to the point of exhaustion. You are less effective and prone to make stupid mistakes. If you're too tired to drive home, have someone come and pick you up, or call a taxi. Perhaps you should get a hotel room for the night. If you've been working late to finish up a project and need time to recuperate, request to take the next day off.

#96 Back Me Up On This

As you turn on your computer to finish up a year-long project, you notice something a little unusual ... nothing appears on the screen except a little message: "The Infector strikes again!"

What's Wrong?

- You never purchased a virus program.

- You didn't take the time to back up your files, either.

- Years of work are now unrecoverable.

- Crying won't bring it back.

- You might as well say good-bye to your project (and your promotion).

Some Success Strategies:

Backup your data files on a regular basis. Install a virus-protection program, and take extra precautions when dealing with files coming from outside the company. Consider making hard copy printouts of important documents and storing them off-site along with an electronic backup. If you've lost data and failed to do the above, don't despair just yet. Oftentimes your data still exists, but may not be easily accessible. Have your system looked at by a professional.

#97 Hit And Run

You dropped a cup of coffee in the lunchroom, and quickly ran away to avoid cleaning it up. For one thing, you're extremely busy, and for another thing ... isn't that what the janitors get paid for?

What's Wrong?

☞ Slip happens.

☞ The clean-up crew hates you.

☞ Being self-centered *and* clumsy is a terrible combination.

☞ It's dangerous.

☞ Someone might have witnessed it.

☞ And they wonder why the floor is always sticky.

Some Success Strategies:

Be considerate of others, and take the responsibility of cleaning up after yourself, especially if you've created a situation that may cause unsafe conditions. Do your share in maintaining good housekeeping throughout your work environment. Always report accidents and mishaps to the appropriate people, whether or not they were caused by you or someone else.

#98 Jack-Of-All-Trades

They call you "Mr. Fix-It." When the copier breaks down, you come running to the rescue with a wrench and a letter opener. Eventually you give up and call for repairs.

What's Wrong?

- You don't know what you're doing.
- The problem may get worse.
- It's not your job.
- You get dirty.
- You're wasting time.
- You may be violating service warranties.
- You might get the shock of your life.

Some Success Strategies:

Don't try to fix things you're not qualified to work on. Always inform the office manager or technical support if equipment is faulty. However, do place service calls that you have been authorized to make. Leave your tools at home. Request that unreliable equipment be upgraded or replaced. Make sure it's plugged in and turned on. If all else fails, read the instructions.

#99 I've Been Asking Myself That For Years

When others ask you what you do for a living, you respond with vague answers. In fact, you're not even sure what you really do.

What's Wrong?

- You appear incompetent and unfocused.//
- It's unimpressive.
- Your self-worth is questioned.
- Your position looks unneeded.
- You have to refer to your business card to remember your job title.
- You're missing opportunities to "sell" yourself and your company.

Some Success Strategies:

Learn to capitalize on these opportunities to market yourself and your job position. Create a list of accomplished tasks, mastered skills, and future goals. Then, create a personal "mission statement," and memorize it! See how your individual achievements affect the company's bottom line. Always appear as if you have a sense of purpose, even if you don't think you do. Clarify your job description with the original job posting.

#100 Just Like Home

Decorating your cubicle with items from home gives it that "personal" touch. Your new curtains don't go very well with the office carpet, but they give you plenty of privacy when you're watching TV.

What's Wrong?

- The office decor is being violated.
- Someone may steal valued personal items off your desk.
- They might start charging you rent.
- Your work area is becoming an eyesore.
- It's unprofessional.
- No one has to guess what your home looks like—it's in plain view.

Some Success Strategies:

Don't overly crowd your work space so that it affects your own productivity or causes you to be disorganized. Think twice before bringing things to work that are inappropriate, overly expensive, too personal, or distracting to others. Consider limiting personal items to family photos, certificates, personal mission statements, simple gifts from vendors, and other business-related knickknacks.

#101 Prankly My Dear...

You think everyone just loves your practical jokes; however, your boss didn't seem very amused about the whoopee cushion antic during the board meeting.

What's Wrong?

- Tricks are for kids.
- You may inadvertently humiliate someone.
- You're causing distractions and making others unproductive.
- Your pranks may be dangerous and/or destroy company property.
- It's unprofessional.
- Revenge is sweet.

Some Success Strategies:

Practical jokes may be admissible in some working environments, however, never pull a joke that could possibly cause injury to another person or that could cause damage to company property. Think before you act. If you have to question yourself whether or not it is a good idea, it probably isn't.

Summary

Stupid is as stupid does. If you can remember this, perhaps you won't find yourself in the land of *stupid* as often.

Take an honest look at how you conduct yourself around the office. See if there's room for improvement. See if you've done any of the *stupid* things in this book.

Focus on the success strategies. You'll surely find some tip that can make you a better employee. And a better person.

Good luck, and I wish you many outstanding performance reviews, memorable office parties, and all the cherished work relationships you can handle.

About The Publisher

Richard Chang Associates, Inc. is a diversified organizational improvement consulting, training, and publishing firm based in Irvine, California. They provide a wide range of products and services to organizations worldwide in the areas of organizational development, quality improvement, team performance, and learning systems. The Publications Division of Richard Chang Associates, Inc., established to provide individuals with a wide variety of practical resources for continuous learning in the workplace or on a personal level, is pleased to bring you this book.

RICHARD
CHANG
ASSOCIATES

Richard Chang Associates, Inc.
Publications Division
15265 Alton Parkway, Suite 300
Irvine, CA 92618
(800) 756-8096   (714) 727-7477
Fax: (714) 727-7007
www.richardchangassociates.com

Additional Resources From Richard Chang Associates, Inc. Publications Division

Practical Guidebook Collection

Quality Improvement Series

Continuous Process Improvement
Continuous Improvement Tools, Volume 1
Continuous Improvement Tools, Volume 2
Step-By-Step Problem Solving
Meetings That Work!
Improving Through Benchmarking
Succeeding As A Self-Managed Team
Satisfying Internal Customers First!
Process Reengineering In Action
Measuring Organizational Improvement Impact

Management Skills Series

Coaching Through Effective Feedback
Expanding Leadership Impact
Mastering Change Management
On-The-Job Orientation And Training
Re-Creating Teams During Transitions
Planning Successful Employee Performance
Coaching For Peak Employee Performance
Evaluating Employee Performance
Interviewing And Selecting High Performers

High-Impact Training Series

Creating High-Impact Training
Identifying Targeted Training Needs
Mapping A Winning Training Approach
Producing High-Impact Learning Tools
Applying Successful Training Techniques
Measuring The Impact Of Training
Make Your Training Results Last

Workplace Diversity Series

Capitalizing On Workplace Diversity
Successful Staffing In A Diverse Workplace
Team Building For Diverse Work Groups
Communicating In A Diverse Workplace
Tools For Valuing Diversity

High Performance Team Series

Success Through Teamwork
Building A Dynamic Team
Measuring Team Performance
Team Decision-Making Techniques

Guidebooks are also available in fine bookstores.

Additional Resources From Richard Chang Associates, Inc. Publications Division

Personal Growth And Development Collection
Managing Your Career in a Changing Workplace
Unlocking Your Career Potential
Marketing Yourself and Your Career
Making Career Transitions

101 Stupid Things Series
101 Stupid Things Trainers Do To Sabotage Success
101 Stupid Things Supervisors Do To Sabotage Success
101 Stupid Things Salespeople Do To Sabotage Success
101 Stupid Things Business Travelers Do To Sabotage Success
101 Stupid Things Employees Do To Sabotage Success

Training Products
Step-By-Step Problem Solving TOOLKIT™
Meetings That Work! Practical Guidebook TOOLPAK™
Continuous Improvement Tools Volume 1 Practical Guidebook TOOLPAK™

Packaged Training Programs
High Involvement Teamwork™
Continuous Process Improvement

Videotapes
Mastering Change Management**
Quality: You Don't Have To Be Sick To Get Better*
Achieving Results Through Quality Improvement*
Total Quality: Myths, Methods, Or Miracles**
  Featuring Drs. Ken Blanchard and Richard Chang
Empowering The Quality Effort**
  Featuring Drs. Ken Blanchard and Richard Chang
Optimizing Customer Value*
  Featuring Richard Chang
Creating High-Impact Training*
  Featuring Richard Chang

Total Quality Video Series And Workbooks
Building Commitment**
Teaming Up**
Applied Problem Solving**
Self-Directed Evaluation**

* Produced by American Media Inc.   ** Produced by Double Vision Studios